Contents

How many times did Henry VIII marry?

The **Tudor** family ruled Britain from 1485 to 1603. The first Tudor king was Henry VII, who seized power from Richard III at the Battle of Bosworth Field. He was succeeded by his son, Henry VIII. Henry VIII's children, Edward, Mary and Elizabeth, ruled after him.

Monarchs in Tudor times rarely married for love. Often they married to link up their families to other rich and powerful families both from England and from other important countries. Henry VII married Elizabeth of York, who was the daughter of an earlier King of England. His son, Henry VIII, had six wives.

The most married monarch

Henry VIII (1491-1547) ruled from 1509 to 1547. In 1509 he married the Spanish princess Catherine of Aragon. Catherine gave birth to a daughter, Mary, in 1516. But Henry longed for sons. Henry's quest for a male **heir** led him to divorce Catherine and marry Anne Boleyn, in 1533. With her he had another

daughter, Elizabeth. But he fell out with Anne too. She was beheaded in 1536. Just eleven days later, he married Jane Seymour. In the next year she did give him a son – Edward – but she herself died soon after.

Portraits as evidence

Many portraits of Henry VIII exist. This one was painted by Hans Holbein.

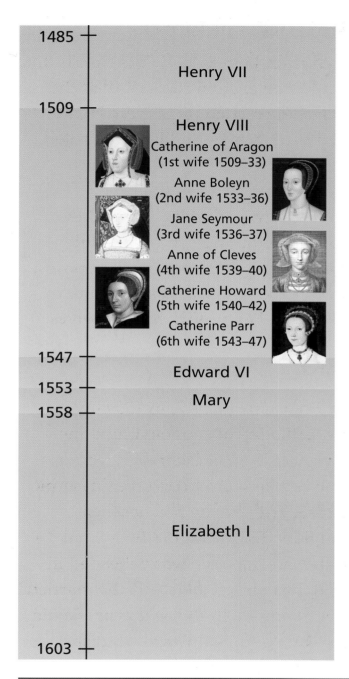

1485

Henry VII

1509

Henry VIII
Catherine of Aragon
(1st wife 1509–33)
Anne Boleyn
(2nd wife 1533–36)
Jane Seymour
(3rd wife 1536–37)
Anne of Cleves
(4th wife 1539–40)
Catherine Howard
(5th wife 1540–42)
Catherine Parr
(6th wife 1543–47)

1547

Edward VI

1553

Mary

1558

Elizabeth I

1603

That left Henry free to marry Anne of Cleves, the sister of a powerful German prince. But they divorced after only six months. By this time Henry was 49. His next wife, Catherine Howard, was thirty years younger than him.

The young Catherine was unfaithful to him and she was executed in 1542. Finally in 1543 Henry married Catherine Parr, who was still his wife when he died in 1547. No English king has ever been married as many times as Henry.

Exploring further

The Heinemann Explore CD-ROM will give you information on Britain and the wider world in Tudor Times. From the Contents screen click on the blue words to find out about the Tudor kings and queens and their people.

What was Henry VIII like as a person?

It is hard to know what people in history were really like. But we can look at pictures of them, and read what other people wrote about them, then try to decide for ourselves. We have to remember too that people in history, like people today, sometimes changed a lot during their lives.

Many portraits of Henry VIII were painted during his lifetime and these show us what he looked like. We can also read descriptions of Henry that were written at the time by people who met him.

A young man

Description of Henry VIII, written by an Italian when the king was about 30 years old:

He is extremely handsome. Nature could not have done more for him. He is much handsomer than any other king... It is the prettiest thing in the world to see him play, his fair skin glowing through his shirt.

Middle age

This portrait of Henry was painted in 1520. The king was about 30 years old. He appears much younger than on page 7, which was painted several years after this one.

HENRICVS VIII REX
ANGLIE

Ill health

A portrait of Henry VIII, painted by Hans Holbein in the 1530s. The king is dressed formally. His face is beginning to show the effects of health problems.

'Every inch a king'

Henry was obviously an attractive man. He looked 'every inch a king', at least until his later years. Then he became fatter and troubled by illnesses. But as a young man, he was a fit, sports-loving person who loved books and music too.

Henry took being king seriously, and he had to work hard at it. But for him, the best part of the job was winning fame and glory. Lord Mountjoy, one of his **courtiers**, said: 'Our king does not desire gold or gems or precious metals, but virtue [and] glory'.

Exploring further – Portraits of a king

Use the CD-ROM discover more about what the king was like. To see more portraits follow this path:

Contents > Pictures > Key People and Events

Click on one of the pictures to make it bigger. A caption will tell you what the picture shows.

What did Henry VIII do all day?

From 1509 to 1547, Henry VIII was the most powerful person in England. He had servants and **courtiers** to make his life comfortable. He also had advisers, or **ministers** who helped him to govern his kingdom.

The role of a king

Nowadays, **Parliament** and the Government make the laws of the land. In Henry VIII's time things were different. As king he was very powerful, but so were some of his leading **noblemen**. Henry had to make sure they obeyed him, and kept control in their parts of the country. He also had to make sure that people paid enough **taxes** to pay the ministers and govern the country.

All work and no play?

Henry still had some time to enjoy himself. As a young man he loved to hunt and ride and play sports like tennis. He liked to have interesting people around him too.

 Hampton Court Palace

At one of his palaces – Hampton Court, just outside London – as many as 1000 people might come to stay at one time. This is Hampton Court Palace today.

Thomas Wolsey (1475-1530) (Cardinal Wolsey)

Wolsey was the son of a butcher from Ipswich in Suffolk. When he became **Lord Chancellor** in 1515 he was the king's most powerful minister. The taxes he raised to pay for Henry's foreign wars made him unpopular with the people. He fell from power in 1529 when he failed to persuade the Pope to allow the king to divorce Catherine of Aragon.

Some days, the king's noble guests might **joust** with him in the 'tiltyard'. Or they might watch plays in the Great Hall, or go to services with him in the Chapel Royal. On other days, he stayed in his **Privy Chamber** to talk with his ministers and discuss and sign important papers.

Henry was also very interested in religion. When Henry came to the throne, England was **Catholic** and the Pope in Rome controlled the Church. The king opposed the **Protestant** ideas of Martin Luther, which had led to a split within the Church. Seeing Henry as an **ally** against these Protestant ideas, the Pope gave him the title 'Defender of the Faith' in 1521.

Exploring further – The king's ministers

Cardinal Wolsey was just one of the king's ministers. The CD-ROM contains information about the lives of some of the others. Follow this path:
Contents > Biographies
You will find biographies of some of Henry VIII's ministers, including Thomas More and Thomas Cromwell. Click on their names to read about them.

Why did Henry divorce Catherine of Aragon?

Catherine of Aragon

Catherine was the daughter of King Ferdinand and Queen Isabella of Spain. She had once been married to Henry's older brother, Arthur, but he had died.

Catherine married Henry when he became king in 1509, and at first they appeared happy. In 1516, Catherine gave birth to a daughter, Mary. By the late 1520s, Henry believed she was getting too old to have another child and began to consider divorce.

In **Tudor** times, divorces were rare. If a king wanted a divorce, he had to get permission from the Pope in Rome. He was the head of the **Catholic** Church, and at that time England was a Catholic country. When Henry asked Pope Clement VII if he could divorce Queen Catherine, the Pope refused.

The need for a son and heir

But why did Henry *want* to divorce his first wife? The real reason was that Catherine had not given him a son. Like most European rulers at that time he was worried about what would happen to his kingdom after he died, and believed that only a strong male could control the powerful **noblemen**. Although Catherine gave birth to four sons, they all died as babies. In 1531 Henry left her, although she stayed in England until she died in 1536.

Thomas Cromwell (c1485–1540)

Thomas Cromwell was Henry VIII's chief **minister** from 1534 to 1540. He played a big part in the English **Reformation**. He organized the closing down of the **monasteries**, such as Fountains Abbey in North Yorkshire, shown here. This made the king very rich, but made many of the king's courtiers dislike Cromwell. In 1540 they whispered to Henry that he should not trust Cromwell. The king listened and Cromwell was executed.

Henry's defiance of the Pope changed his country forever. A new 'Church of England' was set up, with the **monarch** as its leader. Henry was given his divorce by the new Archbishop of Canterbury, Thomas Cranmer, in 1533. This Reformation in England meant that Henry was now allied with the **Protestants**, who also opposed the Catholic Church.

Exploring further – The Reformation

To discover more about Henry's quarrel with the Pope follow this path:
Contents > Exploring > Change and Influences > From Catholic to Protestant
Click on Written Sources on the left of the page to see an extract from the English Prayer Book.

Did marrying Anne Boleyn or Jane Seymour solve Henry's problems?

In the late 1520s King Henry VIII started thinking he needed a new wife. He badly wanted a son to take over from him when he died and his first wife, Catherine of Aragon, had not given him a male **heir**. His eye fell on a much younger woman, Anne Boleyn.

Anne Boleyn

Born in 1507, Anne came from a **noble** family. In January 1533 he secretly married her. Anne was then crowned queen, just before she gave birth. Henry prayed for a son but the child was a girl, Elizabeth.

Anne was never popular at the **Tudor** court. Henry grew more impatient for a son. His impatience meant that he was more likely to listen to rumours whispered by his **courtiers**. These included a rumour that Anne was a witch. Finally in May 1536 he had her executed at the Tower of London.

 Henry with Jane Seymour and their son Edward.

An heir to the throne

Henry was already in love with another young woman. She was Queen Anne's **lady-in-waiting** – Jane Seymour. Henry married her eleven days after Anne's execution. On 12 October 1537, she at last gave Henry a son. But Jane herself died only twelve days later. Henry was heartbroken.

Would Henry marry again?

Henry now had a son and heir. But in Tudor times, one son was often not enough. Many children died before they became adults. If Edward died, then Henry had no second son to take his place. Henry's quarrel with the Pope had left England with many powerful enemies. By marrying a relative of a foreign ruler, England could become friends with that ruler's country. It looked as if Henry would marry again.

 Exploring further – Anne Boleyn and Jane Seymour

To find more information about Anne Boleyn and Jane Seymour click on Search on the top panel of the Contents page. Pick Anne Boleyn or Jane Seymour from the keywords on the next page and click on Enter. The screen will now show a list of pages on the CD-ROM that mention the two queens. Click on the names of the pages to find out what they show.

Why did the marriage to Anne of Cleves fail?

By the early 1500s, the **Catholic** Church had become very rich. Too many Church officials were more concerned about money than their religious duties. Men like Martin Luther, a German priest, suggested ways to change or 'reform' the Church. The highest Catholic officials took little notice. So these protesters or **Protestants** set up their own churches.

Was Henry VIII a Protestant?

Some people in England were Protestants, although Henry VIII was not one of them. But in the 1530s he quarrelled with the Catholic Pope who had refused to grant him a divorce from Catherine of Aragon. As a result Henry split England away from the Catholic Church and set up the new Church of England.

Europe divided

Two powerful Catholic rulers did not like what he had done with the Church in England. They were Francis I of France and Emperor Charles V of Spain. In 1538 rumours spread that they were going to invade England together.

 A Protestant view

This Protestant picture dates from 1545. It shows the Pope with a monster that represents the Catholic Church. This was a time of bitter religious arguments.

Anne of Cleves

Henry had not seen Anne before her arrival in England but he had read reports about her. They were not very good. "I hear no great praise either of her personality or her beauty," said one. Anne was very different from the fun-loving Henry.

Henry tried to make links with Protestant rulers who were not friends of Francis, Charles or the Pope. One was a German prince, Duke William of Cleves. He had an unmarried sister in her twenties – Anne of Cleves. By marrying Anne the king could win the duke's friendship in any wars with Francis and Charles.

Henry goes ahead

Anne arrived in England in December 1539. Henry was very disappointed, but it was too late to back out. On 6 January 1540 Henry's fourth marriage went ahead.

The Catholic invasion that Henry feared never happened. The king had no more need of a friendship with the Duke of Cleves. That gave him a perfect reason to end the marriage. In July 1540 he divorced Anne. He gave her two houses and £500 per year. She stayed in England until her death in 1557.

Exploring further – Martin Luther

The Protestant Reformation affected all of Europe in different ways. It was begun by Martin Luther. To read more about him follow this path:
Contents > Biographies > Martin Luther

Why did Henry marry Catherine Howard and Catherine Parr?

In the 1530s Henry VIII stopped England from being a fully **Catholic** country. But many of his **courtiers** kept their Catholic beliefs. Meanwhile, some others became **Protestants**. The Catholics and Protestants became enemies at court. By marrying a Catholic or a Protestant, Henry would show whose side he was on.

Catholic Catherine

In 1540 Henry fell for Catherine Howard, who belonged to a powerful Catholic family. In July 1540 the fifty-year-old king made Catherine his fifth wife. The marriage only lasted until February 1541. That was when Henry had her executed for being unfaithful to him.

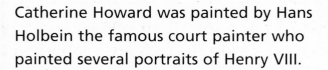

Catherine Howard

Catherine Howard was painted by Hans Holbein the famous court painter who painted several portraits of Henry VIII.

Protestant Catherine

In July 1543 Henry married his sixth wife, Catherine Parr, a well-educated Protestant woman from court. In December 1543, she persuaded him to bring together his children – Mary, Elizabeth and Edward – at court for the first time. In 1547 Henry died, survived by his last wife. Catherine remarried and had a daughter.

Catherine Parr

In 1544, while Henry was away leading an invasion of France, Catherine Parr even ruled the country for three months.

Why did Henry marry six times?

His main aim was to make sure that the **Tudors** would keep on ruling England after he died. Henry lived at a time when the **monarch** had to control powerful families to keep his grip on power. Marriage helped Henry to build alliances with foreign rulers and powerful courtiers.

Henry believed that only a boy could inherit his kingdom. But his son Edward ruled for only six years before he died. Henry's first daughter, Mary Tudor, claimed the throne and reigned for six years before Queen Elizabeth I (1533-1603), Henry's daughter to his marriage to Anne Boleyn, inherited the crown. Elizabeth ruled for 45 years and many now believe she was a more successful ruler than her father. Elizabeth herself said, "I know I have the body of a weak and feeble woman. But I have the heart and stomach of a king. And of a king of England too."

Exploring further – The Tudor Dynasty

The CD-ROM carries lots of information about the other Tudor monarchs – Henry's children. To discover more about their reigns try searching using their names as keywords: Edward VI, Mary I and Elizabeth I. You can find out how to search the CD-ROM in the box on page 13.

What were the differences between the lives of rich and poor people in Tudor times?

How did money affect people's lives?

 In 1577 a clergyman called William Harrison wrote a detailed *Description of England*. This is how he divided up the English people:

We in England divide our people into four sorts. First there are the gentlemen. After the King, the chief gentlemen are the prince, dukes, marquises, earls, viscounts and barons. These are called ... lords and **noblemen**. After them are knights, esquires, and last of all are those who are simply called gentlemen.

Second to the gentlemen come the **citizens**. They live in the cities, and probably do important jobs there.

Third come the **yeomen**. They are freeborn Englishmen and own a certain amount of land.

The fourth and last sort of people in England are day labourers, poor farm workers, some shopkeepers who have no free land ... and all craftsmen such as tailors, shoemakers, carpenters, bricklayers, masons, etc.

 Most **Tudor** poor made their living off the land.

 As **landowners**, the rich did not work for wages, and had servants to run their homes. Many of their big houses still stand today.

Luxury and hardship

Most Tudor people lived in country villages rather than in towns or big cities like London. Everyone helped to produce the nation's food, drink and clothing. In contrast a small number of rich people led more comfortable lives.

Unemployment problems

During the Tudor period, the population rose very fast but the number of jobs did not go up with it. And although the cost of living kept rising, wage-earners did not always get rises too. As a result, the number of the jobless and poor reached record levels. To try to make ends meet, some of them were forced to turn to begging or even to crime.

Exploring further – Everyday life

This path on the CD-Rom will allow you to explore everyday Tudor life:
Contents > Exploring > Everyday Life
You will then be given a choice of topics: Rich and poor; Children and education; Food, holidays and entertainment.

How comfortable were the lives of rich Tudor people?

Before **Tudor** times, the homes of very rich people were more like castles than houses. They were designed to be safe from attackers. By 1500, the new cannons could break down even the thickest walls. So **noblemen** decided that if their homes could not be safe, they might as well be comfortable. There was a craze for home improvement and new building.

In England, King Henry VIII closed down all the wealthy **monasteries** of the **Catholic** Church. Then he sold many of them to rich people, who turned them into very grand homes for themselves and their families.

New trends

Noblemen and gentlemen used timber and plaster, stone and even brick for their building. Glass was now cheaper than before. So big houses' windows grew to a great size and number. Many houses were also fitted with ornamental chimneys, to take away smoke from the fireplace. This is Hardwick Hall in Derbyshire.

Beautiful homes

A description of Tudor town houses, written by Alessandro Magno, an Italian visitor, in 1562:

Inside, houses have beautiful wooden carvings. They have tapestries on the walls. The floors are covered in straw. They have tin dishes full of flowers and sweet-smelling herbs by the windows.

Comfort

This picture shows the inside of a house of quite a rich Tudor person. Yet it had no running water, no electric light, few soft chairs with backs or arms, and the only heat came from log fires.

In early Tudor times, big houses had no upstairs and downstairs. But they had very high ceilings, with a hole in the roof for the smoke from a big fire to escape through. In winter, everyone in the house had to huddle around the fire together – people did not have their own rooms to go to. That all changed with the coming of chimneys. Later Tudor houses had several smaller rooms instead of one large hall. Each room had a fireplace, with the smoke going up separate chimneys.

Exploring further – Tudor homes

The Digging Deeper section of the CD-ROM allows you to find out more about the topics that interest you:
Contents > Digging Deeper > Houses and homes > Manors and mansions gives details about the homes of rich Tudor people.

What can inventories tell us about the lives of people at this time?

In **Tudor** times, when someone died, an '**inventory**' or list of his or her possessions was made. Poor people's inventories were not very long. Some owned only a table, a bench, and a few sacks of straw to sleep on. Some poor families even lived under the same roof as their pigs and cows. Their homes were made mainly of wood, and had no glass in the windows. Instead they used linen, soaked in oil to make it transparent.

The homes of the rich

In contrast to the living conditions of the poor, richer people now had big glass windows. With more light flooding into their rooms, they bought furniture that was beautiful to look at. The best-decorated room was usually the **parlour**.

A gentleman's inventory

John Lawson lived in Chester. He was quite wealthy. An inventory listed his possessions and what they were worth. These are some of the items in it (s means shilling; d means pence):

In the hall One iron fireplace, with all the parts belonging to it, 6s 8d.
A drawing table with a carpet, a bench and three buffet stools 13s 4d.
One table, 1 carpet, 1 bench, 2 chairs with a little chair, and 1 box for salt 13s 4d.
One cupboard with a chest and a pair of tables 18s.
Eleven cushions 4s.
One dagger with a hanger 5s.
In the parlour One standing bed with 1 feather bed, 1 pair of woollen blankets, 2 coverlets, 1 covering, 1 bolster, 1 pillow, with woollen hangings 22s.

Oak beams and glass windows decorate this house in Essex that a Tudor clothes merchant built in 1500.

Improvements all round

William Harrison wrote, in his *Description of England*, in 1577 that the homes of both the rich and poor now had more furniture than in the past. Even workmen and farmers "have learned to decorate … their well-made beds with tapestry and silk hangings, and their tables with carpets and fine cloth."

Modern historians have looked closely at **wills**, left by dead people. These wills show that Harrison was right – by the end of the Tudor period more ordinary people were using beds, and maybe they had a chest or two to store things in. Also at this time, people were starting to use 'proper' tables and chairs, rather than folding tables and benches.

Exploring further – Reconstructing Tudor times

Much of the information we have about Tudor life comes from inventories. It helps us to work out what the insides of Tudor homes were like. On the CD-ROM, you can see what modern artists think Tudor homes may have looked like. Follow this path:
Contents > Pictures > Everyday Life
Click on the pictures to make them bigger.

What was life like for poor people in Tudor times?

There were a lot of poor people in **Tudor** times. Some of these were people who worked but still could not earn enough money to look after their families, or were too ill or disabled to work. Some could not find jobs at all and others, called **vagrants**, lived by begging or stealing from others.

Deserving poor

The very old, the very sick, orphans and widows were called the 'deserving' poor. They 'deserved' the help they got from their families, their neighbours, or from the local church because they could not work themselves. Anyone healthy was expected to find work. But there was no longer enough work to go round.

Children

Children from poor families had to work or beg from a very early age. They lived in the **slum** areas of towns, with many families crammed into badly built houses. In the country they lived in one-roomed cottages or shacks. The very poorest families had no homes, and slept on town streets or under country hedges.

 Illness

Tudor medicine could be brutal, as this painting of an operation shows. Poor people were unlikely to get any help at all when they were sick.

Begging

A family of beggars. Some parents injured their children so they would earn more money begging.

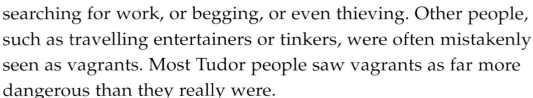

Vagrants

Some poor people were called **vagabonds** or vagrants. These were people who travelled around searching for work, or begging, or even thieving. Other people, such as travelling entertainers or tinkers, were often mistakenly seen as vagrants. Most Tudor people saw vagrants as far more dangerous than they really were.

Deserving poor – the Fulborne family

Alexander Fulborne and his wife Agnes lived in Norwich. They were both 40 years old in 1570. Alexander had trained as a tailor but could not find work. Agnes knitted to make money while their daughters, aged seventeen and twelve, spun wool. They were given **alms** of 2d (2 pence) per week and were described as very poor in the records.

Exploring further – Village wisdom

The CD-ROM contains information about how ordinary people lived. Follow this path to find out about life in villages:
Contents > Exploring > Village wisdom
Click on the pictures on the left of the screen to find out what they show.

The Government takes action

Before **Tudor** times, the Government gave no help to the poor. Tudor Parliaments made '**Poor Laws**' in 1495, 1531, 1536, 1547, 1549, 1552, 1563, 1572, 1576 and 1597. The first of these laws were very harsh. England's rulers thought that the poor and jobless were just being lazy. So, by the Poor Law of 1531, disabled beggars were to be whipped if they strayed outside their home area. And by the law of 1572, **vagabonds** over 14 could be whipped and burned through the right ear. By 1603 the laws were more helpful. Now work had to be found for the healthy and local communities had to look after the old, the sick and the poor.

Vagrants

Thomas Harman, a **Justice of the Peace**, in 1567 writes how some Tudor people saw **vagrants**.

I thought it my duty to tell you of the wicked and detestable behaviour of all of these ragged rabble who – under the pretence of great misery, disease or disaster – manage to gain **alms** from good people in all places.

Food for the poor

In this painting by the Dutch painter Pieter Brueghel, bread is being given to the deserving poor. Rich people often left money in their **wills** to be spent on giving bread to the poor on a particular day each year.

Changing fortunes – Humphrey Gibbons

Humphrey Gibbons was arrested as a vagrant in New Romney, Kent in 1596. He said that in 1586 he had owned a large farm. He had been forced to sell it because of rising prices and bad harvests. He worked as a labourer for three years until he could afford to buy another small farm. In 1596 the harvest failed and he was forced to become a travelling labourer again.

Ford's Hospital almshouse in Coventry today.

Almshouses

One of the ways in which the local people could provide for the poor was through almshouses. These were built to house the deserving poor. Wealthy people often gave money to pay for almshouses to be built and repaired. We know this because people often left money for the almshouses in their wills and these wills have survived. You can still see Tudor almshouses in many towns today.

Exploring further – Tudor children

Poverty in Tudor times affected adults and children. To discover more about Tudor children follow this path:

Contents > Digging Deeper > Tudor Children

Then click on one of the blue topic headings to find information.

How different were the lives of rich and poor people?

Life in **Tudor** times was very different from life in Britain now. Even the lives of very rich Tudor people would have been uncomfortable to us.

People's attitudes were also different then. Today we believe in **equal opportunities** for men and women. Children are respected too. In Tudor times, in both rich and poor families, men and boys were believed to be 'superior' to women and girls – and children were treated very harshly.

Entertainment

The theatre was popular entertainment for wealthy and ordinary people. Ticket prices ranged from 1d (d stands for pence) in the area around the stage to 6d in the balcony above the stage. Ordinary workers could afford the cheaper areas, although not the very poor. Seats in the best balconies were too expensive for anyone but the rich.

Everyday life

In this painting you can see both rich and poor people. The rich are sitting at the table while the poor are working in the kitchen.

How some Tudor people saw things

Obviously, it was much more pleasant to be rich than to be poor in Tudor England. Poor people led hard lives, and until the late 1500s they got little help from the Government. Their homes, health, clothes and food were all worse than those of the rich.

Many accepted that it was just 'the way things were'. In their opinion, this was how God had created the world, and how he wanted it to stay – with everyone fixed in his or her place. On Earth some people would always be rich, they thought, and a lot more would be poor. But in heaven, there would be no differences. We may not see things in the same way today, but rich and poor people still lead very different lives.

Exploring further – William Shakespeare

Shakespeare's plays were popular with rich and poor people. Read about his life by following this path:

Contents > Biographies > William Shakespeare

In the Written Sources section [Contents > Written Sources] you can find extracts from some of Shakespeare's plays.

Timeline

1485	Henry Tudor fights Richard III to win the Battle of Bosworth and becomes King Henry VII
1491	Henry VIII born
1492	Christopher Columbus reaches America
1509	Henry VIII becomes King of England and marries Catherine of Aragon
1516	Mary born
1517	Martin Luther starts the Protestant Reformation in Germany
1521	Pope gives Henry the title 'Defender of the Faith'
1522	Ferdinand Magellan of Spain is the first person to sail right around the world
1529–1539	English Reformation, including closing of the monasteries. Church of England established.
1533	Henry divorces Catherine of Aragon and marries Anne Boleyn. Elizabeth born.
1536	Anne Boleyn beheaded. Henry marries Jane Seymour.
1537	Edward born. Jane Seymour dies.
1540	Henry marries and divorces Anne of Cleves and marries Catherine Howard
1543	Henry marries Catherine Parr
1547	Death of Henry VIII. Boy-king Edward VI takes over from his father.
1552	New Prayer Book in English is used in church
1553	Edward VI dies. Catholic Mary becomes Queen of England.
1554–1558	England and Wales become Catholic again
1556	Philip II becomes King of Spain
1559	Protestant Elizabeth crowned Queen of England
1564	William Shakespeare born
1568	Mary, Queen of Scots flees to England
1577–1580	Francis Drake sails around the world
1584	Sir Walter Raleigh tries to set up Roanoke colony in America
1587	Mary Queen of Scots executed after nearly 20 years under arrest
1588	Spanish Armada defeated
c1588–c1613	William Shakespeare writes his plays
1603	Elizabeth I dies and the Tudor dynasty ends

Glossary

ally   a close friend or supporter – can be a person or a country

alms   money given to the poor for food and clothes

Catholic   member of the Catholic church – the only Christian church in western Europe before the Protestant Reformation, with the Pope as its head

courtiers   people who spent time at the royal court as companions or advisers to the king or queen

equal opportunities   when all people, whether men, women or children, or different nationalities all have the same chances

heir   someone to be the next ruler

inventory   a list of possessions, e.g. someone's household furniture and belongings

joust   a competition between knights, on horseback and armed with long poles called lances

Justice of the Peace   a local government official, first set up in Elizabethan times

lady-in-waiting   a female servant who looks after a queen or princess

landowner   someone who owns land and earns a living from the people who work on the land

Lord Chancellor   the monarch's chief advisor, who has charge of the courts of law

ministers   members of the government who work for and advise the king

monarch   king or queen

monastery   a religious place where monks live together

noblemen (or nobles)   rich and important men who help the ruler to rule the country

Parliament   the House of Lords and the House of Commons, which met in London to advise the ruler and make laws

Poor Laws   laws made by Parliament to try and force poor people into work, and to stop people being vagrants

Privy Chamber   The king's private chamber or room

Protestant   member of one of the new churches set up in the 1500s to replace the Catholic Church

Reformation   the setting up of Protestant churches in Europe (including England) as a protest against certain wrongs in the Catholic Church

slum   a very run-down area

taxes   money collected by the church and king to pay for buildings or to equip the army and navy

Tudor   The family name of Henry VII, Henry VIII and his children, and also the term we use to describe the period in which they lived

vagabond   a person with no home and often no job who wanders from place to place. Some vagabonds turned to crime to survive.

vagrant   the same as a vagabond

will   the written wishes of a person about sharing his or her property among people after he or she dies

Index